LIBRARY OF CONGRESS

Prints and Photographs

AN ILLUSTRATED GUIDE

LIBRARY OF CONGRESS WASHINGTON 1995

This publication was made possible by generous support from the James Madison Council, a national, private-sector advisory council dedicated to helping the Library of Congress share its unique resources with the nation and the world.

The text for this guide was written by Bernard F. Reilly, Jr., with extensive contributions and research by C. Ford Peatross, Cristina M. Carbone, Harry L. Katz, Verna Posever Curtis, Beverly W. Brannan, Carol Johnson, and Elena Millie.

Photographs were taken by Jim Higgins.

Designers for this guide were Robert Wiser and Laurie Rosenthal, Meadows & Wiser, Washington, D.C.

COVER: John Plumbe, Jr. *The United States Capitol from the East.* Detail. Half-plate daguerreotype, circa 1846. The earliest surviving photograph of the Capitol, Plumbe's daguerreotype shows the Capitol with its old copper-sheathed wooden dome. This work was one of several daguerreotypes of Washington scenes and buildings—including the White House and the U.S. Patent Office—acquired by the Library in 1974.

LIBRARY OF CONGRESS CATALOGING-IN-PUBLICATION DATA

Library of Congress.
      Library of Congress prints and photographs : an illustrated guide.
         p.   cm.
        ISBN 0-8444-0816-6
        ———— ———— Copy 3 Z663 .L459   1994
        1. Prints — Catalogs. 2. Photographs — Catalogs. 3. Prints — Washington (D.C.) — Catalogs. 4. Photographs — Washington (D.C.) — Catalogs. 5. Library of Congress — Catalogs. 6. Library of Congress.
NE53.W3L49   1994
760'.074'753 — dc20   94−17438
                                                        CIP

For sale by the U.S. Government Printing Office
Superintendent of Documents
Mail Stop: SSOP, Washington, D.C. 20402−9328

Contents

Preface

FOR NEARLY TWO CENTURIES the Library of Congress has served as the national library of the United States. In this role it has become custodian of the record of the American people and an unparalleled repository of world history, knowledge, and achievement.

Prominent among the Library's holdings are its pictorial collections. Unique in their scope and richness, these collections today number over 14 million works. These range from watercolor views, portraits, and master prints and photographs to architectural renderings and working drawings, and mass-produced propaganda posters, news photographs, and printed ephemera. For historians, these visual documents are keys to an understanding of the people, events, and achievements that have shaped American and modern European history and the histories of such regions as Latin America, the Middle East, Africa, and Central Asia.

Preserved in the context of a research library, these collections are made available each year to tens of thousands of researchers in the reading room of the Prints and Photographs Division and through telephone inquiries and written correspondence. They also reach millions more through publications, exhibitions, films, and electronic dissemination.

This vital national legacy has been built through the combined efforts of the Congress, an international community of creators and benefactors, and the people of the United States. The Library traces the establishment of its collections to the acquisition by the Congress of Thomas Jefferson's library in 1815. Since Jefferson's time there have been numerous occasions when individuals and organizations have helped advance the Library's efforts to assemble and preserve a comprehensive visual record of the past. (A chronology of the defining moments in the development of the collections appears at the back of this guide.) The collections featured herein are a testament to the success of this public-private cooperative endeavor.

As the twentieth century draws to a close, the Library's strong commitment to the preservation and the accessibility of these collections ensures that they will continue to serve as the raw material from which the American people, and researchers and creators the world over, may fashion an understanding of their past.

STEPHEN E. OSTROW, CHIEF
PRINTS AND PHOTOGRAPHS DIVISION

Dorothea Lange. *Migrant Mother, Nipomo, California, February 1936.* Gelatin silver print. (*Farm Security Administration—Office of War Information Collection*)

SUCCESSIVE PAGES. George Lawrence. *Photograph of San Francisco in Ruins from Lawrence Captive Airship,* detail. Gelatin silver print, 1906. (*Transfer, U.S. Copyright Office*)

PHOTOGRAPH OF
SAN FRANCISCO IN RUINS
FROM LAWRENCE CAPTIVE AIRSHIP
2000 FEET ABOVE SAN FRANCISCO BAY
OVERLOOKING WATER FRONT.
SUNSET OVER GOLDEN GATE.

Introduction

THE PICTORIAL COLLECTIONS of the Library of Congress represent an immense fund of human experience, knowledge, and achievement. Works in these collections touch upon almost every realm of human endeavor: science, art, invention, government and political struggle, and the recording of history.

In these realms, the arts of drawing, printmaking, and photography have served a multitude of purposes over the years. They have been the bearers of information, vehicles of commentary and persuasion, tools in the creative process, and media of artistic expression. All of these roles are represented in the drawings, prints, and photographs in the Library's collections.

These works' value as historical documents is informed and enriched by the circumstances of their creation. As bearers of information, the arts of drawing and printmaking have a long history. Since prehistoric times drawing has been a universal language, used by people to record and, in the process, interpret their surroundings. Printmaking, a much younger art, has provided a means of disseminating drawings and the information they contain. The birth of printmaking in the West six centuries ago coincided with the revival of science and classical humanism in late medieval Europe. Prints and drawings were indispensable to the communication of the new scientific information gathered during the era of exploration that followed.

As time went on, drawings and prints were produced to mark important milestones in the transformation of the American landscape through settlement, urbanization, and industrialization and to display the wonders of its unspoiled regions. In the early years of the nineteenth century artists like John Rubens Smith traveled throughout the United States, recording in pencil and watercolor the cities and towns, mills, bridges, and suburban estates that dotted the countryside during that dynamic age.

Photography, introduced in 1839, eventually superceded the other graphic arts as a medium of historical record. Initially it was hailed as a paragon of factuality. Its images materializing through the action of sunlight on a sensitized surface, the medium supposedly eliminated from the recording process the subjective element of human mediation. People embraced photography as a way of preserving important moments in the course of their lives. The thirty-seven-year-old Abraham Lincoln, soon after winning his first seat in the House of Representatives, sat for a local daguerreotypist at Springfield, Illinois. The portrait, as straightforward as its plainspoken subject, is the earliest known photograph of the Great Emancipator, taken when he had yet to cast his first vote in the Congress.

Attributed to Nicholas H. Shepherd. *Abraham Lincoln.* Quarter-plate daguerreotype, circa 1846. *(Gift of Mary Lincoln Isham)*

John Rubens Smith. *Mill on the Brandywine, Delaware.* Watercolor on laid paper, circa 1830. *(John Rubens Smith Collection. Gift of the Madison Council and Mrs. Joseph Carson)*

Fidelity to appearances notwithstanding, photography actually allows considerable room for subjectivity. Any number of creative decisions made by the photographer in the process of making a photograph, such as the choice of subject, perspective, equipment, and the moment of exposure, all introduce a measure of interpretation. In her portraits of a number of the luminaries of her age, the British photographer Julia Margaret Cameron used the technical variables of the medium to express, as she put it, "the greatness of the inner as well as the features of the outer man." In her portrait of Alfred Lord Tennyson, one of several intimate studies included in a Cameron album owned by the Library, the photographer exploits the optical peculiarities of her camera lens and the physical properties of the albumen printing process to convey the brooding genius of the Victorian poet.

It was photography's literal rather than evocative qualities that have endeared the medium to scientists, explorers, historians, and others with a vested interest in observed detail. In the decades following the American Civil War photographers were employed to accompany a succession of congressionally funded exploring expeditions and geological surveys of the American West and Southwest. Expedition commanders often published reports of their surveys illustrated with large albumen print photographs of peculiar or magnificent features of the wilderness terrain. Photographs like Timothy O'Sullivan's view of New Mexico's Cañon de Chelle, produced on the George M. Wheeler Expedition, were intended to both inform and dazzle the public—as well as the expedition's federal sponsors—back East.

OPPOSITE. Julia Margaret Cameron. *Portrait of Alfred, Lord Tennyson.* Albumen silver print, 1876.

Photography has also been used extensively to record architecture and the built environment. One of architectural photography's acknowledged masters was Frances Benjamin Johnston. Possessed of a prescient interest in the humbler structures of American vernacular architecture, Johnston spent the latter part of her career documenting the vanishing buildings of the Old South. In her photograph of the whitewashed outbuildings of West Martingham in rural Talbot County, Maryland, Johnston has preserved some of the more rudimentary products of American architectural creativity.

In architecture as in portraiture the best records are not always the most literal ones. Drawing often surpassed photography in capturing the essence of architectural and engineering accomplishments, and in conveying a sense of the human experience of these works. By far the most ambitious engineering venture of its era, the construction of the Panama Canal surmounted enormous obstacles—environmental, political, and technical—before its completion in 1914. In his series of drawings and lithographs of the project the American printmaker, illustrator, and critic Joseph Pennell captured the superhuman scale of this achievement.

Pennell's Panama Canal series exudes an unabashed national pride in the American accomplishment of carv-

Frances Benjamin Johnston. *West Martingham Outbuildings, St. Michael's, Talbot County, Maryland.* Gelatin silver print, 1936. *(Carnegie Survey of the Architecture of the South)*

LEFT. Joseph Pennell. *Building Miraflores Lock.* Lithograph, 1912. *(Gift of Joseph and Elizabeth Robins Pennell)*

OPPOSITE. Timothy O'Sullivan. *Ancient Ruins in the Cañon de Chelle, New Mexico.* Albumen silver print, 1873.

ing a waterway to link two great oceans. The canal was not only a marvel of American ingenuity but a symbol of the emergence of the United States as the major power in the Western Hemisphere. As an expression of that moment, Pennell's work is, more than a record, a commentary on the new international order of his day.

As Joseph Pennell recognized, images possess an innate advantage over text as vehicles of commentary and persuasion. Their immunity to the constraints of reasoned argument have made them valuable tools in politics and advertising. The Library's extensive collection of political prints and posters consists of works created to advance the goals of societies, governments, and movements and those which voiced the doubts of their critics.

Among the most penetrating social commentaries ever created are the etchings of the Spanish artist Francisco Goya. Employed at the court of Charles IV, Goya witnessed from a privileged vantage point the corruption of a decadent regime, the foibles and superstitions of his own society, and the atrocities committed by Napoleon's occupying troops upon his countrymen. His prints present a deeply cynical picture of his times, as a dark age pervaded by human evil.

The darkest days of American president Andrew Jackson's administration were a golden era for political cartoons in the United States. During Jackson's second term, thousands of caricatures were issued by opponents of his fiscal program and the corrupt spoils system of government patronage. Cartoons from the period, most of them issued anonymously, reflect the high pitch of public feeling on these issues.

Optimism, not doubt, is the pervasive tone in the Library's holdings of advertising posters and prints. Since the early nineteenth century, commerce has used printmaking to present its objects of desire—be they soap, entertainment, or political candidates—in a favorable light. Posters (printed images executed on a bold, attention-grabbing scale) were pioneered by American circuses and political campaigns. Joseph Morse's tour de force of the genre, from the Library's rich collection of early American circus posters, is over eleven feet long. It was probably meant to be posted on the side of a building, to herald the arrival of a troupe of traveling circus performers.

In the twentieth century, with large-scale industrial development and the advent of an international consumer economy, advertising has become a weapon of mercantile competition. The heat of this competition and a revolution in print-

Francisco Goya y Lucientes. *Lealtad (A Man Mocked)*. Etching and burnished aquatint on laid paper, 1816 or later. *(Caroline and Erwin Swann Memorial Fund Purchase)*

Artist unknown. *The Tory Mill*. Woodcut and letterpress on green wove paper, circa 1834. *(Caroline and Erwin Swann Memorial Fund purchase)*

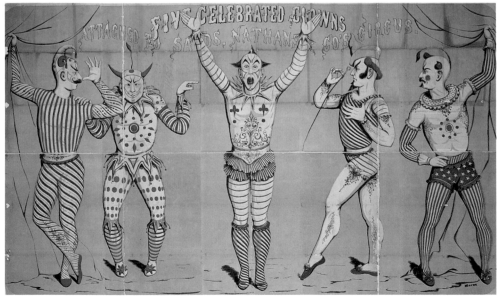

Joseph Morse. *Five Celebrated Clowns Attached to Sands, Nathan Company's Circus*. Woodcut printed in colors by Morse, M'Kenney & Company, 1856. *(Transfer, U.S. Copyright Office)*

ing technology transformed graphic design from a craft into a highly sophisticated profession. Posters and other print advertising by modern manufacturing giants are often the products of corporate identity programs, demographically based marketing strategies, and motivational research. Chicago artist and art director Otis Shepard developed an advertising campaign for the Wrigley Corporation in the 1930s that continues to influence the look of the company's corporate advertising today.

Twentieth-century graphic designers wield a vastly expanded vocabulary of typography, photography, and printing techniques. In his 1938 poster for an exhibition of commercial photography, Czech designer Jan Tschichold applied this vocabulary in the disciplined terms of Bauhaus design, where the forms themselves and the interrelationship of text and image become the primary subject of the work.

Far from the political fray and the engines of commerce, the graphic arts have also played a role in the creative process, as tools in the shaping of the man-made world. Drawing in particular has been instrumental in the making of buildings, bridges, monuments, and other elements of the built environment. For architects and patrons, drawings have provided a means to conceptualize and develop schemes for architectural projects and to impart these schemes to those who constructed them. The U.S. Capitol in Washington evolved through a succession of design competitions and building campaigns, which can be traced in part through architects' drawings which survive in the Library's collections. In his 1811 elevation rendering, Benjamin Henry Latrobe presented a majestic scheme, though one ultimately discarded, for the West Front of the Capitol.

unter mitarbeit des schweizerischen photographen-verbandes

gewerbemuseum basel   ausstellung

der berufsphotograph   sein werkzeug — seine arbeiten

8. mai — 6. juni

werktags	14-19	
mittwochs	14-19	19-21
sonntags	10-12	14-19
eintritt frei		

Jan Tschichold. *Der Berufsphotograph.* Color offset poster, 1938.

Robert Fulton, best known for his invention of the steamboat, elaborated in a series of drawings a number of designs for submarines, torpedoes, and other underwater devices, anticipating by over a century the actual introduction of undersea navigation. Fulton actually built and tested his submarine, or "plunging boat," the *Nautilus,* for Napoleon in France in 1800.

Other inventors have used photography to record works in progress, documenting the arduous, often lurching, progress of experimentation and discovery. Photographic "note-taking" by the Wright brothers, Alexander Graham Bell, and others has yielded today's researchers a detailed record of the triumphs and failures of these pioneers. The Wright brothers systematically photographed the prototypes and tests of their various flying machines. Their historic first powered flight at Kitty Hawk, North Carolina, in December 1903 was one of a number of scenes documented in a collection of about 300 negatives acquired by the Library from the estate of Orville Wright. The camera, operated by an attendant from a nearby lifesaving station, captured their plane on the instant of takeoff. The craft soared to an altitude of 2 feet.

OPPOSITE. Otis Shepard. *Wrigley's Double Mint Chewing Gum.* Color offset poster, 1938.

Benjamin Henry Latrobe. *United States Capitol. Rendered Elevation for West Front with Propylaeum.* Graphite, ink, and watercolor on laid paper, 1811.

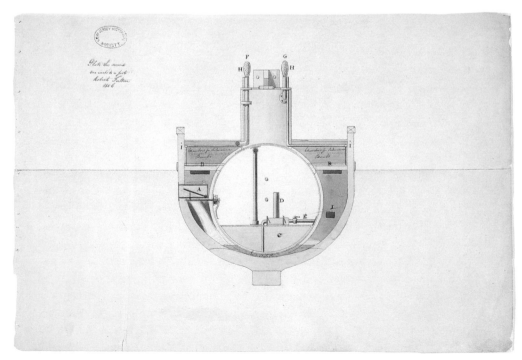

Robert Fulton. *Section Rendering of Submarine or "Plunging Boat."* Graphite, ink, and watercolor on paper, 1806.

The less practical uses of the graphic arts prevail in the Library's holdings of fine prints and master photographs. For almost six centuries artists have found in printmaking a realm where technical process uniquely informs creativity, and have explored the expressive possibilities of the medium as a way of communicating deeper human matters of perception and meaning. Master painters like Rembrandt and Whistler have created substantial bodies of work in printmaking. Among the most masterful and enduring accomplishments in the art is Rembrandt's etching *The Three Trees*, an outstanding impression of which is owned by the Library. In this work Rembrandt uses line, thick and thin, richly overlayed and isolated, to both describe the forms in a landscape and suggest the surrounding space, light, and atmosphere.

In a series of Venetian studies made in 1879 or 1880, Whistler used the same medium in a much different but equally remarkable manner. In *Nocturne*, the artist reserves his line to provide a shorthand description of a few recognizable objects, such as a ship, the church of Santa Maria della Salute, and the island of San Giorgio, allowing the manipulated inking on the surface of the plate to dominate the sheet and provide an atmospheric ambience and sense of mystery.

Photography, the younger-sister art to printmaking, has compiled an equally imposing record of artistic achievement. One of the most ardent early advocates for the recognition of photography as a fine art in the United States was F. Holland Day. His 1898 meditation on Keats's famous line, "Beauty is Truth, and Truth Beauty," part of an archive of his work donated to the Library by the photographer in 1934, exemplifies Day's poetic use of his medium.

Much different in effect and approach is the work of Austrian-born modernist Lisette Model. In her *Running Legs*, one of a series of street scenes taken in New York shortly after the photographer emigrated there, Model uses the expressive possibilities of the medium to capture the spirit of urban life in the early 1940s.

The drawings, prints, and photographs in the Library's collections are documents rich in information, and laden with the ideas, values, and opinions of their makers and their times. The portfolios that follow include a selection of works chosen to highlight some of the major research strengths of the Library's holdings. These works present a range of viewpoints as diverse as the artists, politicians, journalists, architects, and inventors who created them.

John T. Daniels. *First flight, December 17, 1903. Distance, 120 feet. Time, 12 seconds. Orville Wright at controls.* Modern gelatin silver print from glass negative.

OPPOSITE TOP. Rembrandt Harmenszoon van Rijn. *The Three Trees.* Etching, dry-point, and engraving on laid paper, 1643. *(Gardiner Green Hubbard Collection)*

OPPOSITE BOTTOM. James McNeill Whistler. *Nocturne.* Etching and dry-point, printed in brown ink on laid paper. First state of five, circa 1879. *(Joseph and Elizabeth Robins Pennell Collection)*

ABOVE LEFT. F. Holland Day. *Beauty Is Truth, Truth/Beauty.* Platinum print, before 1897. *(Gift of the photographer in the name of Louise Imogen Guiney.)*

ABOVE RIGHT. Lisette Model. *Running Legs, New York.* Gelatin silver print, 1940–41.

Portfolio 1: An American Gallery

THE DRAWINGS, PRINTS, AND PHOTOGRAPHS preserved in the Library's collections constitute a composite picture of the life and peoples of the United States, a picture of extraordinary richness, diversity, and nuance. During the last two centuries American draftsmen and photographers have observed their contemporaries, taking in the famous and the obscure alike and portraying the full spectrum of the American identity. These artists' works capture more than mere appearances. They convey the values, concerns, spirit, and ways of life of their subjects as well.

Today the Library holds archives of the work of portrait photographers Mathew Brady and Arnold Genthe, Lewis Hine's photographs for the National Child Labor Committee, and the pictorial files of the NAACP (National Association for the Advancement of Colored People).

The Library also houses the photographs of the Farm Security Administration and Office of War Information which, numbering over 300,000 negatives and prints, represent the most comprehensive photographic survey of the lives and occupations of ordinary people ever created. The extensive photographic record of American life during the Great Depression was conceived to generate support for President Roosevelt's New Deal economic and social programs. Aside from its enormous success in this mission, the photographic project directed by Roy Stryker became a laboratory for exploration of the persuasive power of photography.

These and the Library's other documentary holdings constitute a wealth of primary evidence for historians of material culture and social history.

John Rubens Smith. *Design for a Certificate issued by the Philadelphia Association for the Relief of Disabled Firemen.* Watercolor and graphite on wove paper. Circa 1830.

A versatile figure in the American art community during the first half of the nineteenth century, John Rubens Smith was an accomplished painter, an experienced printmaker, and a leading educator during a formative period in the development of American art. His many drawings of American scenes and people combine a high standard of draftsmanship and a fidelity to actual appearances remarkable for their time. Smith's drawing for a benevolent society certificate contains a wealth of rare detail on American firefighting technology and equipment during the Jacksonian period, from the elegantly functional pumpers to the colorful uniforms of the engine companies. (*John Rubens Smith Collection. Gift of the Madison Council and Mrs. Joseph Carson*)

Mathew B. Brady. *Horace Greeley.* Half-plate daguerreotype, circa 1850.

The eccentric New York editor Horace Greeley, known for his directive, "Go West, young man," personified the ebullient spirit of American Republican politics in the 1850s. In his hobnail boots, long coat, and stove-pipe hat, Greeley was a fixture of the New York scene. Mathew Brady made a career of photographing such public figures (for the exorbitant sum of three to five dollars apiece), and he displayed these portraits in his fashionable gallery at Broadway and Fulton Streets. His portrait of Greeley is from an archive of over 300 Brady Studio daguerreotypes acquired by the Library in 1920. *(Transfer, U.S. Army War College)*

ABOVE LEFT. Anonymous. *A Seamstress.* Sixth-plate daguerreotype, circa 1853.

The unidentified subject of this daguerreotype sits behind an industrial model Grover and Baker sewing machine. Whether originally produced as a promotion for the machine's manufacturer, an illustration of the clothing industry at the time, or a portrait of a proud seamstress displaying the tools of her trade, this daguerreotype is one of the few surviving visual documents of working women in the United States before the Civil War.

ABOVE RIGHT. Arnold Genthe. *Street of Gamblers.* Toned gelatin silver print, circa 1898.

Arnold Genthe's photographic studies of the people and streets of San Francisco's Chinatown before the earthquake of 1906 reveal something about Asian-American life and contemporary attitudes toward this immigrant group at the turn of the century. Emigration of the Chinese to the West Coast of the United States accelerated rapidly in the waning years of the nineteenth century. The Chinese were attracted by the inexhaustible demand for labor in the American West and driven abroad by the violence and hardships of the Opium Wars. Genthe focused on the insular aspects of Chinatown life, eliminating by the deft retouching of his negatives the telegraph lines and other signs of western technology. Genthe's studio archive of negatives and prints was acquired by the Library of Congress shortly after the photographer's death.

LEFT. Edward S. Curtis. *Shows as He Goes.* Gelatin silver print, circa 1907.

From 1906 to 1927 Curtis traversed the western United States and British Columbia, studying and photographing the vanishing native American peoples and their many cultures. His project, largely financed by J. Pierpont Morgan, resulted in a monumental twenty-volume opus *The North American Indian*, which was illustrated with 1,500 photogravures. The Library owns a complete copy of this work, as well as an estimated 2,800 of Curtis's photographs. *(Transfer, U.S. Copyright Office)*

RIGHT. Gertrude Käsebier. *The Red Man.* Platinum print. Negative produced around 1900.

Unlike Edward Curtis, who methodically sought to record the dress, life, and customs of native Americans, Gertrude Käsebier photographed only a few Indians, Sioux members of Buffalo Bill's Wild West troupe whom she invited to pose in her New York studio. Käsebier was the finest portraitist of the American Pictorialist School, and in *The Red Man* her mastery of the idiom draws forth from the subject a strong psychological presence, at once imposing and reserved. *(Gift of the photographer)*

Lewis Hine. *Shrimp and Oyster Worker, Biloxi, Miss. February 1911.* Gelatin silver print. Manuel, the five-year-old shrimp-picker shown here, spoke no English. At the time this photograph was taken, he had already worked for a year in this tedious and hazardous occupation. The abusive child labor practices of industry in pre-World War I America were the targets of the National Child Labor Committee, and photographer Lewis Hine was one of the committee's greatest publicists. For fifteen years he crisscrossed the United States documenting the practices of the worst offenders. The Library holds the papers of the National Child Labor Committee, including the reports, field notes, correspondence, and over 5,000 of Hine's photographs and negatives. *(Gift of the National Child Labor Committee, in honor of the committee's fiftieth anniversary)*

Ben Shahn. *Years of Dust.* Color lithograph poster, 1936.

A distinguished painter, illustrator, and photographer, Ben Shahn designed only a few posters during his long career. *Years of Dust,* produced for the Resettlement Administration (which later became the Farm Security Administration), is believed to have been his first. In conveying a sense of the despair of the impoverished Dust Bowl farmer, Shahn's poster was an apt piece of propaganda for the agency, which strove to ease the hardships of the American agricultural community.

ABOVE LEFT. Carl Van Vechten. *Zora Neale Hurston.* Gelatin silver print. 1938.
Now called the "literary grandmother" to black women writers, author and anthropologist Zora Neale Hurston was a major figure in the Harlem Renaissance of the 1920s and 1930s. Carl Van Vechten's portrait was taken the year after Hurston's most important novel, the folk romance *Their Eyes Were Watching God,* was published. Van Vechten, a writer, critic, and amateur photographer, was an ardent advocate of African-American music and letters. He bequeathed to the Library of Congress an archive of approximately 1,400 photographs of the artists, literati, and other celebrities of the period, from Josephine Baker to William Faulkner. *(Gift of the photographer's estate)*

ABOVE RIGHT. Russell Lee. *Buck Dancer at a Square Dance, Pie Town, New Mexico, June 1940.* Gelatin silver print.
The photographic record of everyday life produced under the Farm Security Administration during the Great Depression succeeded in generating support for New Deal economic and social programs and became a cornerstone of modern American documentary photography. *(Transfer, Office of War Information)*

Ansel Adams. *Toyo Miyatake.* Gelatin silver print, 1943.

Under the Civilian Exclusion Order of 1942 over 100,000 western seaboard residents of Japanese descent were evacuated from their homes and relocated in internment camps in the interior. The order was conceived during the hysteria following the Japanese attack on Pearl Harbor, in an effort to prevent sabotage of America's war effort. Toyo Miyatake, a Japanese photographer who was interned at the Manzanar camp, was photographed by Ansel Adams, who visited Manzanar at the invitation of the camp's director. Adams's visit resulted in the famous landscapist's only photo essay, the book *Born Free and Equal* (1944). Two copies were sent to Franklin Delano Roosevelt by Secretary of the Interior Harold Ickes, as part of the secretary's campaign to end the internments. After copies of the book were publicly burned in protest Adams deposited his Manzanar negatives in the Library of Congress, to safeguard the record for better times. *(Gift of the photographer)*

Richard Avedon. *The Chicago Seven.* Gelatin silver print, 1969.

A photographer highly esteemed in the world of art and commerce, Richard Avedon photographed the Chicago Seven defendants during their tumultuous and protracted trial for the disruption of the 1968 Democratic National Convention in Chicago. The defendants were charged with conspiracy for their part in the antiwar demonstrations staged at the convention. The subjects are, from left: Lee Weiner, John Froines, Abbie Hoffman, Rennie Davis, Jerry Rubin, Tom Hayden, and David Dellinger.

Portfolio 2: Pictorial Journalism

THE FIRST PHOTOGRAPH published in an American newspaper—actually a photomechanical reproduction of a photograph—appeared in the *Daily Graphic* on March 4, 1880. Before that time it was common practice for American editors to enlist artists to sketch and report on news events, from steamboat explosions to the battles of the Civil War. It was actually not until 1919, with the launching of *New York's Illustrated Daily News*, that American newspapers began to feature photographs routinely. The lighter cameras and "faster" lenses introduced in the 1920s brought about a revolution in news photography and ushered in the age of photojournalism.

The Library preserves several premiere archives of pictorial journalism, including several thousand drawings by Civil War artist-correspondents, the studio archives of several early news photographic agencies such as the Bain News Service and the National Photo Company, and the morgues of such publications as *Look* magazine, the *New York World-Telegram and Sun*, and *U.S. News and World Report*. These collections offer historians vivid documentation of the newsworthy events of yesterday, as well as providing insights into journalistic practice.

Alfred Waud. *Wounded Escaping from the Burning Woods in the Wilderness, May 6, 1864.* Pencil and Chinese white on brown paper.

If not the bloodiest battle of the Civil War, the Battle of the Wilderness may have been the most terrifying. It was fought in early May 1864 in the dense, dry pine forests west of Fredericksburg, Virginia. In his sketch for the editors of *Harper's Weekly* Waud captured the panic overwhelming disabled soldiers on the ground and the ambulance corps charged with their care, as brushfires burned out of control. The Library's collection of Civil War drawings, prints, and photographs make up the nation's most comprehensive visual record of that war. *(Gift of J. Pierpont Morgan)*

D. B. Woodbury and Alexander Gardner, for the Mathew B. Brady Studio. *Military Bridge, Across the Chickahominy, Virginia, Maryland, June 1862*. Albumen silver print (published 1865).

The grandfather of American war correspondents, Mathew Brady used the fortune he had made from his successful New York portrait studio to place dozens of photographers, like Alexander Gardner, in various parts of the theater of operations during the Civil War. By his own estimate Brady spent nearly $100,000 on this pioneering endeavor. After the panic of 1873, Brady was temporarily rescued from financial ruin by an act of Congress authorizing the purchase of his daguerreotypes for the nation. An archive of over 7,500 of the Brady Studio's Civil War glass negatives came to the Library in 1943.

William Glackens. *A Street Scene at Tampa City.* Gouache and ink over graphite on wove paper, 1898.

The Spanish-American War, though brief, was a source of enduring legends in American military history, from the explosion of the battleship *Maine* in Havana harbor to Theodore Roosevelt's famous charge at San Juan Hill. In this drawing by the young painter William Glackens, American troops parade through Tampa City en route to transport ships waiting to take them to Cuba. Dispatched to the front by *Colliers'* magazine to cover the war, Glackens was one of several young members of New York's Ash-Can school who made a living as artist-reporters. The drawings produced on this assignment were donated to the Library by the artist's son. *(Gift of Ira Glackens)*

ABOVE LEFT. Photographer unknown (National Photo Company). *President Calvin Coolidge Facing Press Photographers, 1924.* Recent gelatin silver print from original glass negative.

Calvin Coolidge entered the White House at the dawn of the "communications age." The early twentieth century saw the rise of photographic agencies like the Bain News Service, the National Photo Company, and others, formed in the early years of this century to satisfy the increasing demand for magazine and newspaper pictures. Acutely aware of the potential usefulness of the press to his administration's goals, Coolidge became one of the most photographed presidents of the era. Archives of both the Bain and National Photo firms, which combined total nearly 250,000 negatives and prints, are among the Library's extensive photojournalistic holdings. (*National Photo Company Collection*)

ABOVE RIGHT. Photographer unknown (Bain News Service). *Emma Goldman on a Street Car, 1917.* Recent gelatin silver print from original glass negative.

This candid photograph was probably taken during one of the many strikes or antiwar demonstrations in which the anarchist and feminist was active during World War I. Two years later, at the height of the Red Scare, Goldman was deported to the Soviet Union, to return in 1934, disenchanted with the Soviet experiment and with the violent political repression in Stalin's Russia. No doubt the photographer saw the irony in the patriotic Uncle Sam poster visible here behind the determined ideologue's head. (*Bain News Service Collection*)

Walker Evans. *Floyd Burroughs' Farm*, from *Hale and Perry Counties and Vicinity, Alabama, 1935–1936*. Gelatin silver prints in two albums.

Evans's unpublished photographic essay on the homes and families of three Alabama sharecroppers grew out of an assignment James Agee was given to write an article on cotton tenancy for *Fortune* magazine's "Life and Circumstances" series. At that time Evans was at the peak of his artistic powers, but was under contract to the New Deal's Resettlement Administration. Impressed with Evans's careful and unsentimental studies of the rural poor, Agee persuaded the agency to lend Evans to the magazine on the condition that the photographs produced on the assignment would become government property. In fact, the photographs were never published by *Fortune*, but the collaboration resulted in the book *Let Us Now Praise Famous Men*. (*Transfer, Office of War Information*)

TOOL HOUSE, CHICKEN HOUSE

HOUSE FROM REAR

Toni Frissell. *Col. Benjamin O. Davis, Air Base at Rametti, Italy, March 1945.* Recent gelatin silver print from original negative. Davis was commanding officer of the 332d Fighter Pilot Squadron, the only black pilot unit in the American armed services during World War II. He was photographed at the unit's base in southern Italy by Toni Frissell who, after the war, resumed her distinguished career as fashion and portrait photographer for magazines such as *Vogue, Harper's Bazaar, Life,* and *Town and Country.* When Frissell retired from professional photography in 1971 she donated the archive of her career's work to the Library of Congress. *(Gift of the photographer)*

TOP. James Karales. *Civil Rights March, May 1965.* Recent gelatin silver print from original negative. Published in *Look* magazine.

During the 1960s the struggle for civil rights raged in the American South. *Look* magazine photographer James Karales captured in epic, haunting terms a watershed event in that struggle: the 1965 march on Birmingham, Alabama. Three hundred black Americans and many white priests, ministers, nuns, and rabbis participated in the fifty-four mile march to protest discriminatory Jim Crow laws. Karales's photograph accompanied an article about the role of organized religion in the desegregation campaign. The *Look* magazine photographic morgue includes nearly 5 million photographs, negatives, and transparencies. (*Look Magazine Collection. Gift of John and Gardner Cowles*)

BOTTOM. Photographer unknown (Black Star Agency). *Tenth Regiment 7 Division Infantrymen Awaiting U.S. Helicopters at Ben Tre, Vietnam, January 1970.* Recent gelatin silver print from original negative.

Vietnamization was the term used for the phased withdrawal of U.S. combat troops in Vietnam and their replacement by native forces (ARVN). Here a newly formed South Vietnamese unit awaits transport to the landing zone of an operation between Saigon and the Cambodian border. (*Gift of the U.S. News and World Report Corporation*)

Danny Lyon. *Gonaïves, February 9, 1986.* Gelatin silver print, printed in 1989.

The revolt that ultimately toppled Haitian dictator Jean-Claude ("Baby Doc") Duvalier is believed to have originated in the rural village of Gonaïves in January 1986. By chance, photographer Danny Lyon was in Haiti at that moment. Long familiar with the people of the republic, Lyon published his book *Merci Gonaïves,* in which this photograph appeared, as a counterpoint to largely superficial media coverage of the event, which had presented the popular revolt as gratuitously and hideously violent. The photographer's journal entry from the day this photograph was taken reads: "Firing continues at night. Outside of Port-au-Prince it is quiet. The Haitians I know believe they have their revolution.... Television is discussing events freely for the first time in Haitian history."

Portfolio 3: Politics and Propaganda

FROM PROPAGANDA POSTERS TO DRAWINGS by contemporary editorial cartoonists to designs for national monuments, the Library's collection is the most comprehensive existing resource for the comparative study of the political uses of art. Effective means for the inexpensive and rapid dissemination of images, prints and posters have been perennial tools of political interests and causes. Less fugitive creations, like public monuments and government buildings, provide visible expression of more enduring political beliefs and ideals. These works provide today's historians a valuable index of the political ideologies and opinions of societies past.

Thomas W. Strong. *Union*. Wood-cut printed in colors on paper, 1848.

From early on, American presidential campaigns bore a striking resemblance to another popular spectacle: the circus. Mexican war hero Zachary Taylor's 1848 campaign borrowed a leaf from the circus publicists' book by introducing to the pageantry of the political contest large colorful woodcut posters. This example, the earliest known presidential campaign poster, was produced even before Taylor clinched the Whig party's nomination. Taylor's celebrity was so great at the time that the artist did not feel compelled to even include the candidate's name on the work. (*Transfer, U.S. Copyright Office*)

OPPOSITE. James Gillray. *The Grand Coronation Procession of Napoleone the 1st Emperor of France*. 1804. Etching with watercolor on wove paper. Published by Hannah Humphrey, London, January 1, 1805.

James Gillray was among the most popular, prolific, revered, and reviled print satirists of the golden age of English caricature. During this period, revolution rocked France, bringing the brilliant and charismatic military leader Napoleon Bonaparte to power, and sending shock waves of fear and anxiety across the Channel. Bonaparte became a favorite target of British satirists, and Gillray responded in characteristically spectacular fashion with this parody of the pomp and ceremony surrounding the imperial coronation.

LEFT. Käthe Kollwitz. *Aufruhr (Uprising)*. Etching, drypoint, and aquatint on wove paper, 1899.

Much of the art of modern social protest traces its roots to the work of German artist Kathe Kollwitz. One of a cycle of prints and drawings which the young Kollwitz produced on the theme of peasant revolt, her impassioned *Uprising* hearkened back to the *Bauernkrieg* (literally, "farmers' war") of the sixteenth century while portraying the dire straits of agricultural laborers in contemporary Germany. *(Pennell Fund purchase)*

RIGHT. Boardman Robinson. *Europe 1916*. Lithographic crayon, ink, and gouache on paper, 1916.

World War I was viewed by American socialists as the product of international competition between industrial capitalists. Artists like Boardman Robinson, John Sloan, and others used the leftist journal *The Masses* as their platform to take an adamantly pacifist stance amid mounting bloodshed in Europe and the inexorable drift of American public opinion toward involvement in the conflict. The Library's collection of American po-litical drawings is the most extensive in existence, numbering over eight thousand original works. *(Ben and Beatrice Goldstein Foundation Collection. Caroline and Erwin Swann Memorial Fund purchase)*

James Montgomery Flagg. *I Want You for the U.S. Army.* Offset lithograph, 1917. Flagg's memorable and remarkably intrusive recruiting poster was produced under the auspices of the Division of Pictorial Publicity of the Committee on Public Information during World War I. Flagg was one of an army of American illustrators mobilized by Charles Dana Gibson for the war effort. Under Gibson's direction, the division was extraordinarily successful in galvanizing American public opinion in favor of U.S. involvement in the European conflict, shoring up Woodrow Wilson's effort to make the world safe for democracy. (*Gift of the Talbot County Public Library*)

P. Sokolov-Skalia. *The Result of Fascist Culture.* Poster, hand-stenciled with letterpress text, 1939.

The Soviet news agency TASS played a crucial role in supporting armed resistance to the Nazi invasion of the USSR in 1939. Massive German armored forces easily overwhelmed Soviet border defenses and rolled to the gates of Moscow itself, before being turned back by Allied soldiers. Weekly, TASS issued posters designed to stoke patriotic fervor and anti-German feeling, which it displayed in news agency offices in the major Soviet cities. This work condemns Nazi crimes against Russian culture, asserting that "Deathless is the genius of the Russian nation." The Library owns what is probably the most extensive surviving set of the TASS posters. *(Gift of the Packer Outdoor Advertising Company)*

OPPOSITE. Leni Riefenstahl. *Erwin Huber war bester Europäer im Olympischen Zehnkampf (Erwin Huber was the leading European in the Olympic Decathlon).* Gelatin silver print, 1936. The outstanding German filmmaker Leni Riefenstahl is today remembered chiefly for her work in support of the Third Reich. Riefenstahl produced and presented to Adolph Hitler at Christmas 1936 an album of still photographs of scenes from the summer 1936 Olympiad. The album, including this image of the German discus thrower Erwin Huber, is now part of the Library's collections. It documents the creation of Riefenstahl's award-winning film *Olympia,* and the cult of sport and physical fitness which was fundamental to Nazi ideology. *(Transfer, Department of Defense)*

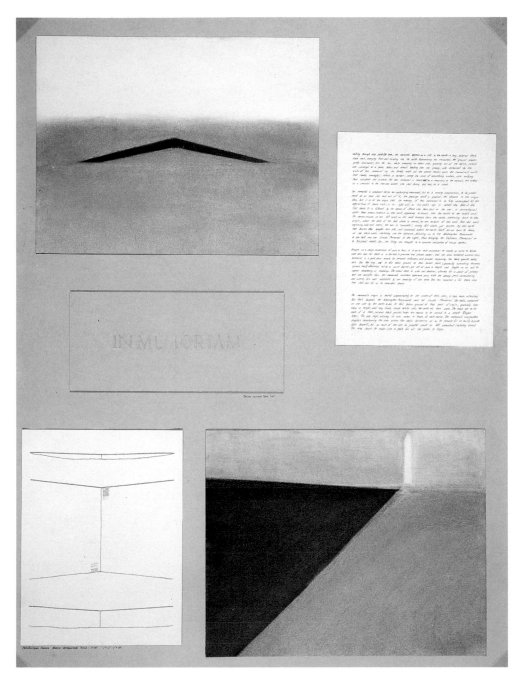

Maya Ying Lin. *Vietnam Veterans Memorial Competition.* Presentation panel in mixed media on paper, 1981.

The Vietnam Veterans Memorial, originally designed as a student project by Maya Lin at Yale University Architectural School, has become a profound national symbol. Lin envisioned a black granite wall, in the shape of a *V*, on which the names of the American military dead and missing would be inscribed. The architect hoped that "these names, seemingly infinite in number, [would] convey the sense of overwhelming numbers, while unifying these individuals into a whole." Since its unveiling, the work—popularly known as "the wall"—has become a point of reference for all American memorials. Maya Lin's drawing is included in the archive of the competition. *(Gift of the Vietnam Veterans Memorial Committee)*

OPPOSITE. Paul Szep. *Vietnam Specters.* India ink on scratchboard. Published in the Boston *Globe*, 1967.

During the 1960s, extensive news coverage of the Vietnam War contributed to growing antiwar sentiment in the United States. The strength of that sentiment divided the nation and the Democratic Party, and convinced President Lyndon Baines Johnson to withdraw from the 1968 election campaign. Two-time Pulitzer Prize-winner Paul Szep created a powerful and unforgettable image in this depiction of LBJ haunted by the ghosts of dead American soldiers. *(Caroline and Erwin Swann Collection)*

Portfolio 4:
The World
at Large

S UPPORTING THE LIBRARY'S ROLE as a repository of world knowledge, the pictorial collections document the peoples, lands, and cultures of the major countries throughout the world. In assembling this record, the Library gives particular attention to the influence and interests of the United States abroad and to individuals and matters of global, regional, or international importance. Regions outside of Western Europe—in particular Latin America, Africa, the Middle East, Eastern Europe, and the Far East—are especially well represented. These holdings provide valuable insights into the history of these regions, and into the ways in which they and their peoples have been perceived by or represented to Americans and Western Europeans.

LATIN AMERICA, THE CARIBBEAN, AND SPAIN

Courret Hermanos, Fotografos. *Lima. The Public Square on 28 July (Independence Day).* Albumen silver print, probably 1868. During its four or so decades of operation, the Lima firm of Courret Hermanos maintained a high standard of photographic work. This view of Lima's central square, festooned for an Independence Day celebration, is one of nearly 100 superbly printed albumen prints of Peru and Bolivia included in a two-volume souvenir album entitled *Recuerdos del Peru.* The *Recuerdos* contains several views of Lima and its gardens, public works, and elegant buildings, views of smaller towns like Arequipa, Callao, and Arica, and portraits of gauchos, muleteers, bullfighters, and other people of the region. (*Transfer, U.S. Department of State*)

Lima The Public square on 28 July. (Independence Day.)

William Berryman. *Woman Beating Cassava, Jamaica*. Watercolor over gray ink and pencil on wove paper, circa 1808.

The English artist William Berryman spent eight years in Jamaica while the West Indian island was under English colonial rule. During that time he produced over 300 pencil and watercolor studies of the Jamaican people, flora, landscape, and buildings, in preparation for an intended series of engravings. Berryman died before carrying out his ambitious project, but his drawings were preserved in an album recently acquired by the Library. Of all his Jamaican subjects, the artist seems to have had a particular affection for the resident Africans and mulattoes who had been freed when Great Britain ended slavery in her empire.

Eadweard Muybridge. *Ruins of the Church of Santo Domingo, Panama.* Albumen silver print, circa 1875.

In 1875 San Francisco photographer Eadweard Muybridge (later to become famous for his photographs of humans and animals in motion) traveled to the Isthmus of Panama. At that time Panama was part of Colombia, and Colombian President Juan Berrios was attempting to rejuvenate the coffee plantations by granting investment incentives to new and established growers. Muybridge braved the tropical climate and rainforest of much of Central America, photographing points of interest on the route of the Panama Railroad and the Pacific Mail Steamship Company's line. His efforts were financed by the Pacific Mail line, which hoped that publication of the photographs in North America would attract new investors to the region. This view of a group of children in the shell of a Spanish colonial church on the isthmus is from an extensive archive of prints, photographs, and ephemera assembled by the Canal Zone Library. *(Transfer, Canal Zone Library)*

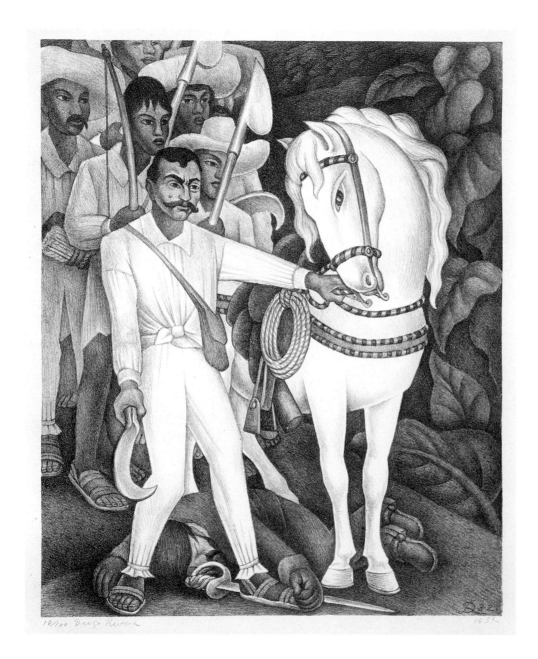

10/100 Diego Rivera 1932

Diego Rivera. *Zapata.* Lithograph, 1932. Artists in postrevolutionary Mexico undertook to enshrine in Mexican history the revolution and its peasant leaders such as Emiliano Zapata. Supported by the large-scale educational programs of the national government, Diego Rivera and others created an art based on indigenous forms accessible to even the less sophisticated members of Mexican society. Lithographs and woodcuts, relatively inexpensive types of prints, played an important role in popularizing this modern art in Mexico. *(Pennell Fund purchase)*

Jack Delano. *Member of a Sugar Cooperative, vicinity of San Piedras, Puerto Rico, January 1942.* Kodachrome transparency.

The Office of War Information carried on the work of the earlier Depression-era Farm Security Administration photographic project in surveying American agricultural and economic conditions and the efficacy of federal programs to improve these conditions. On his assignment to document Puerto Rican sugar growers, Jack Delano used the newly developed Kodachrome color transparency film. The work is part of the archive of over 300,000 photographic images produced under the Farm Security Administration and Office of War Information photographic projects. *(Transfer, Office of War Information)*

Julio E. Suárez. *Fiestas de Carnaval Montevideo 1942*. Color lithograph poster.

When they arrived in Latin America, European, African, and Asian people brought with them diverse cultures, politics, and social mores. Carnival and other festivals became the loci around which this diversity of cultural heritage was blended into a rich, harmonious, and popular expression. The designer of this poster emphasized that each celebration is a work of art in itself, with its own special dances, costumes, dramas, and music, melding a variety of religions, rituals, and cultures. *(Gift of the Packer Outdoor Advertising Company)*

ABOVE LEFT. Photographer unknown (A.B.C. Press Service). *Scene during the Siege of Teruel, Spain. April 1, 1938.* Gelatin silver print.

The Spanish Civil War, which lasted from 1936 to 1939, sparked passionate interest among the international intellectual and political communities. The Communist government of the Spanish Republic was besieged by nationalist forces headed by Gen. Francisco Franco, who was backed by Nazi Germany and Fascist Italy. The war was closely watched around the world, as the first major military contest between left-wing forces and the increasingly powerful and heavily armed Fascists. Here a republican soldier seeks cover on the Plaza de Toros, in Teruel, east of Madrid.

ABOVE RIGHT. Arribas. *18 Julio 1936–1937.* Color lithograph poster, 1937.

The intensity of the bitter conflict between republican and nationalist forces in Spain is reflected in this poster by the pseudonymous artist Arribas. The poster was produced for the two major Spanish labor organizations, the Union General de Trabajo and the Confederacion Nacional de Trabajo. It marked the first anniversary of the date on which nationalist leader Gen. Francisco Franco issued his antirepublican manifesto and launched his devastating military campaign against the Spanish Republic. The poster appeals to the indignation of industrial workers toward foreign-backed aggression in a rousing call to arms for republican volunteers. *(Gift of the Packer Outdoor Advertising Company)*

THE FORMER SOVIET STATES AND THE NEAR EAST

Roger Fenton. *Cavalry Camp, Church Parade.* Albumen silver print, 1855.

The first war extensively recorded by the camera was the Crimean War, which pitted England, France, and Sardinia against Russia in the 1850s over control of the Black Sea province. British photographer Roger Fenton recorded the military camps, officers, soldiers, and landscape of the theater of operations in the Crimea. Not entirely impartial, Fenton's undertaking was sanctioned by the British government, which was anxious to disprove gruesome reports of conditions in the Eastern theater issuing from the war's opponents at home. The prints in the Library's set of Fenton's Crimean photographs were inscribed and titled by the photographer.

Sergei Michailovich Prokudin-Gorskii. *Windmills in the Yalutorovsk.* Recent color print from three-color separation negative, circa 1910.

On the eve of the Russian Revolution Czar Nicholas II of Russia commissioned a photographic survey of his empire by the educator and chemist Sergei Michailovich Prokudin-Gorskii. The product of the imperial charge was a comprehensive travelogue of Russia, Ukraine, Siberia, and the Caucasus and a milestone in the development of color photography.

OPPOSITE. N. V. Bogaevskii. *A Leather Factory in Tashkent.* Albumen silver print, 1871–72.

Military activity in Central Asia continued after the Crimean War. In 1867 Russia extended its control eastward across the Caspian Sea to the largely Islamic region of Turkestan. Populated by a variety of nomadic clans, the region had long been isolated from the rest of the modern world. The first Russian military governor commissioned an encyclopedic photographic survey of the area's peoples, customs, culture, buildings, and monuments, designed to acquaint Westerners with the region, and possibly to serve as an orientation tool for new officials and the home office. The photographs from the survey were assembled in the four-volume *Turkestanskii Al'bom*, of which the Library's copy is one of only seven known sets.

Manœuvre d'une barque de sauvetage à Tira

Abdullah Freres. *Life Saving Brigade.* Albumen silver print, 1893.

The monumental fifty-one-volume photographic survey of the realm of Sultan Abdul Hamid II of Turkey, the last of the Ottoman emperors, was produced under the direction of the Istanbul firm of Abdullah Freres. The work appears to have been conceived by the sultan as a portrait of his empire for the 1893 World Columbian Exposition, but was not exhibited there. It dwells on such accomplishments and westernizing improvements of the regime as the well-equipped military, lifesaving and fire fighting brigades, and life at the lavish imperial court. A copy of the survey was presented by the sultan to the Library of Congress in 1894. *(Gift of H.I.M. the Sultan Abdul Hamid II)*

アメリカ人子供愛図

Yoshitoyo Utagawa. *Picture of Americans' Love for Children.* Color woodcut, 1860. Japanese artists, working in the traditional idiom of the color woodcut, created a fascinating record of the encounter between their civilization and the West following Commodore Perry's opening of Japan to foreign trade in 1853. The Library's extensive collection of Japanese woodcuts includes many portrayals of British, Russian, Dutch, and American naval officers, diplomats and their families. These reflect the novelty of Western dress and ways, such as the Victorians' solicitous treatment of children, to the Japanese of the period. *(Gift of Mrs. Emily Crane Chadbourne)*

9003—Company of Boxers, Tien-Tsin, China.

Photographer unknown (The Whiting View Company). *Company of Boxers, Tien-Tsin, China.* Stereograph, 1901.

The Opium Wars and Boxer Rebellion were tragic consequences of contact between China and the West in the later nineteenth century. Although British and American operations in China during the period are well documented, few photographs of the Chinese Boxer troops survive. Originating in the mid-nineteenth century, the stereograph was an ancestor of the newsreel, affording Americans a window on the remote corners of the globe. The Library's collection of over 30,000 stereographs produced by such firms as Whiting, Underwood and Underwood, and the Keystone View Company spans the 1850s through World War I. (*Transfer, U.S. Copyright Office*)

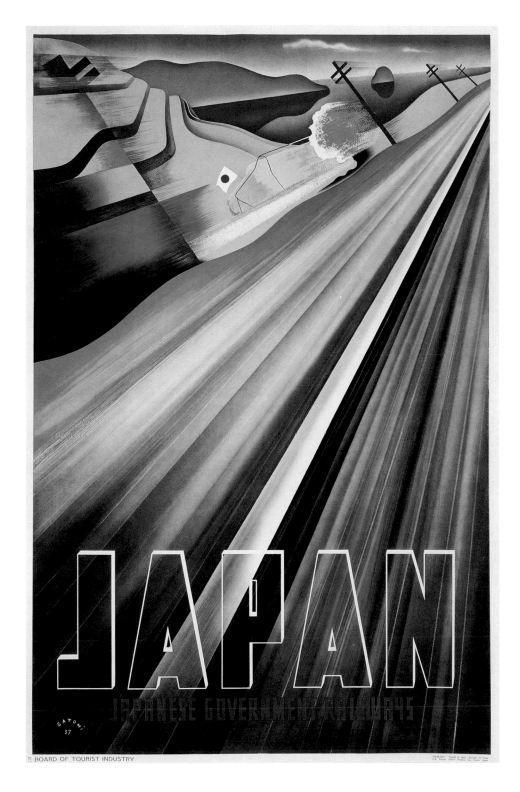

Munetsugu Satomi. *Japan.* Color lithograph poster, 1937.

One of the acknowledged masters of Japanese poster design, Munetsugu Satomi created the vivid illusion of speed in this advertisement for the Japanese railroad. Born in Osaka, Japan, Satomi studied at the Ecole des Beaux Arts in Paris. This poster draws on the stylistic idiom of European Art Deco, indicating the designer's assimilation of the influence of French poster masters.

Louis Haghe, after David Roberts. *Jerusalem from the Mount of Olives, 1839.* Lithograph printed in colors, in George Croly and David Roberts, *The Holy Land, Syria, Idumea, Egypt, and Nubia* (London: F. G. Moon, 1842–49).

The great sacred cities and sites of the Near East were fully illustrated for the first time in the monumental three-volume work by David Roberts, a self-taught Scottish scene painter praised for the accuracy and coloring of his drawings. Belgian printmaker Louis Haghe's portfolio of lithographs made after them were considered quite faithful to the originals and a masterpiece of color lithography.

Lewis Larson. *Surrender of the Mayor of Jerusalem to the British Army, December 9, 1917.* Recent gelatin silver print from stereographic negative.

Jerusalem mayor Hussein Hashim El-Husseini (with cane) walked along the Jaffa Road under a flag of truce made from a hospital bedsheet. At the first British outpost, he surrendered the city to two British sentinels. This image is from an archive of 20,000 photographic negatives documenting people, places, and events of the Middle East from the turn of the century to World War II. *(Gift of Edith and G. Eric Matson)*

Félix Teynard. *Le Kaire. Tombeaux de Sultans Mamelouks* (Tomb of the Mameluke Sultans, Cairo). Salt print photograph, 1851. Published in *Égypte et Nubie, Sites et Monuments les plus Intéressants pour l'Étude de l'Art et de l'Histoire* (Paris: Goupil et Cie, 1858). In the mid-nineteenth century, a growing vogue for tourism led Americans and western Europeans to such exotic places as Greece, the Holy Land, and Egypt. Photographers exploited this trend by producing and marketing series and albums of souvenir views. Félix Teynard's photographic exploration of Egypt and Nubia in 1851–52 produced one of the earliest photographic records of the archaeological sites in this region. The sandy terrain and the weathered faces of the monuments that Teynard photographed are heightened by the surface texture of the photographic paper of the calotype process—one of the earliest processes for producing photographs on paper. *Le Kaire* is from a series of 160 photographs issued originally in installments and then as a complete collection in book form in 1858.

Portfolio 5: Architecture, Design, and Engineering

The Library's architecture, design, and engineering holdings document the full spectrum of American architectural achievement, from the grand tradition of academic classicism, in federal projects like the U.S. Capitol, to the vernacular spirit informing Spanish missions as well as roadside architecture. Through a variety of types of works on paper, among them developmental sketches, measured record drawings, and photographs, the collections document the design process and its products.

Notable among these holdings are the archives of "form-givers," individuals such as Charles Bulfinch, Frank Lloyd Wright, and Raymond Loewy. They and others like them have redefined some aspect of American architecture, design, and engineering and given it new form. Another collection focus is on the introduction and uses in the United States of new building types and technologies, from cast-iron storefronts to steel suspension bridges.

Laura Gilpin. *Rancho de Taos Mission, New Mexico.* Platinum print photograph, circa 1933.
Built in 1772 by Spanish missionaries and native Americans, the Mission Church is an amalgam of European and indigenous building traditions. Made of adobe, a brick composed of straw and mud, the walls slope outward to buttress the structure and to fend off the effects of torrential rains. The Mission Church was recorded in photographs and drawings by the Historic American Buildings Survey in the 1930s and has enjoyed great popularity with artists such as photographer Laura Gilpin and painter Georgia O'Keeffe, both of whom lived nearby. *(Gift of the photographer)*

Front of Boston Library, Franklin place.

Charles Bulfinch. *Front of Boston Library, Franklin place (Tontine Crescent, Central Pavilion).* Graphite and ink on paper, 1793–94. The Tontine Crescent, consisting of sixteen three-story brick houses with a pavilion at the center, was one of the earliest uses of contemporary European town planning principles in the United States. Built in Boston's South End, the crescent was conceived as one-half of a planned ellipse, in the center of which was to have been a small park. Although praised by Bulfinch's contemporaries, the project ruined the architect financially and was never completed.

Frank Lloyd Wright. *Perspective Drawing for the Dr. John Storer House, Hollywood, California.* Graphite and colored pencil on paper. 1923.

Perhaps the greatest genius of American architecture, Frank Lloyd Wright experimented widely during the 1920s with new design vocabularies and building systems. One of his few built works of the period, the Storer House was also one of the first to employ a system of precast "textile" blocks, whose three-dimensional surfaces enliven its exterior. *(Gift of Donald Walker)*

ABOVE LEFT. Detroit Publishing Company. *The Woolworth Building at Night.* Gelatin silver print, 1913.

This commercially produced photograph records the opening festivities of what was for seventeen years the world's tallest building, and which remains a symbol of American technological and commercial achievement. The Library also holds architect Cass Gilbert's original 1910 sketch for this building. The photograph is from among over 25,000 images of American cities, towns, and landscapes created by the Detroit Publishing Company between the 1890s and the 1920s. *(Gift of the Colorado Historical Society)*

ABOVE RIGHT. Photographer unknown. *Kewpee Hotels Hamburgs.* Gelatin silver print, 193-.

Roadside architecture is a longstanding genre in the American vernacular tradition. In the 1930s, buildings such as this hamburger stand were state of the art, using the latest in high technology porcelain enamel siding which imparted to such public eating places an efficient and sanitary appearance. Frequently destroyed with the changing times, roadside curiosities such as this often survive only in photographs and drawings. *(Gift of Mrs. Louise Ray)*

Lith of Sarony, Major & Knapp, 449 Broadway, N.Y.

Daniel Badger. Frontispiece, *Illustrations of Iron Architecture* (New York: Baker & Godwin, 1865). Lithograph printed in colors. The Library's collections richly document the development, introduction, and manifold uses of new technologies in the design and building industries of the United States. From the 1850s until after the turn of the century, cast iron was widely and innovatively employed throughout the United States as both a structural and decorative building material. This rare and beautifully illustrated example from the Library's extensive collection of manufacturers' trade catalogs preserves for us the work of New York City's Architectural Iron Works, one of the finest suppliers of cast-iron facades and other architectural elements.

Charles and Ray Eames, for Evans Furniture. *LCW (Lounge Chair — Wood)*. Recent gelatin silver print from original film negative, 1945.

Charles and Ray Eames first experimented with molded plywood during World War II, designing aircraft parts and splints for the U.S. Navy. Adapting their ideas for the postwar market, the Eameses designed for commercial firms such as Evans Furniture an array of products—tables, radios, and their first signature chair, the "LCW" (Lounge Chair—Wood)—in this versatile material. Intended for mass production, the lounge chair was emblematic of the clean lines and good design associated with the "simple living" so strongly desired in the American postwar market. The photograph of the prototype of the chair is from among the estimated 750,000 photographs, drawings, and related materials in the archive of the Office of Charles and Ray Eames. *(The Work of Charles and Ray Eames, Bequest of Ray Eames)*

Raymond Loewy. *Design sketch for the Avanti Automobile.* Fluid marker on paper, 1961. One of the inventors of modern industrial design, Raymond Loewy redefined the look of everything from logos to locomotives. For many years the principal designer for the Studebaker Corporation, Loewy used this drawing in designing the Avanti sedan in February 1961.

Portfolio 6: The American Landscape and Cityscape

Drawings, prints, and photographs from the past two centuries record the topographical and architectural realities, as well as human experience, of the cities, towns, and landscape of the United States. The Library's holdings, particularly rich in American city views and commercial photographs of buildings and streets, are a source of detailed information on the growth and evolution of the American city, the history of urban planning and land use in the United States, and the art of representing landscape.

A unique treasure is the Library's collection of American panoramic photographs, produced between 1860 and 1930. The photographic panorama, a medium friendly to the open spaces and boom towns of the American West, had its heyday at the end of the nineteenth century. Because panoramas are by definition large and fragile, odds did not favor their survival, and the Library's collection of over four thousand panoramas is now the most comprehensive in existence.

City of CHARLESTON S. Carolina

Looking across Cooper's River

William James Bennett. *City of Charleston, South Carolina, Looking Across Cooper's River.* Engraving and aquatint with watercolor, on paper, 1838.

Drawings and prints from the early nineteenth century provide a rich and vivid record of the growth of the United States and the emergence of the young republic. The rapidly changing American landscape and fast-growing cities and towns were recorded by successive generations of artists such as William Birch, John Rubens Smith, August Kollner, Alfred Waud, and the British-trained watercolorist and engraver William James Bennett. The works of these artists now evoke discrete eras in American history from the Federal period to Reconstruction. (*Transfer, U.S. Copyright Office*)

ABOVE. George Barnard. *Landscape—Looking Down the Valley of Running Water Creek from near Whiteside's.* Albumen silver print from two glass plate negatives, 1864.

The bridge, located between Nashville and Chattanooga, had recently been constructed by the Union Army's Department of Engineers. The railroad was essential to the support of the occupying force. This panoramic photograph was made while the photographer was employed by the quartermaster general. *(Orlando Poe Papers)*

OPPOSITE TOP. William Henry Jackson. *Panorama of Marshall Pass and Mt. Ovray.* Albumen silver print, 1890.

Best known for his work with the U.S. Geological Survey in the 1860s and 1870s, Jackson later produced views along various railroad lines to promote tourism. This image was made from four eighteen-by-twenty-two-inch glass negatives, carefully and almost seamlessly joined on one sheet of photographic paper. The print is from an archive of over 20,000 prints and 30,000 glass negatives of Jackson's Detroit Publishing Company. *(Gift of the Colorado Historical Society)*

OPPOSITE BOTTOM. George Lawrence. *Photograph of San Francisco in Ruins from Lawrence Captive Airship.* Gelatin silver print, 1906.

The photographic panorama was ideally suited to capturing the effects of disasters on the cataclysmic scale of the San Francisco earthquake. Taken before the invention of the airplane, Lawrence's panorama was made possible by hooking a camera to a kite (or "captive airship") which then floated high above the smoldering ruins of the city. *(Transfer, U.S. Copyright Office)*

PHOTOGRAPH OF
SAN FRANCISCO IN RUINS
FROM LAWRENCE CAPTIVE AIRSHIP
2000 FEET ABOVE SAN FRANCISCO BAY
OVERLOOKING WATER FRONT.

W. Eugene Smith. Page from *A City Experienced: Pittsburgh, Pa., a Photographic Interpretation.* Gelatin silver contact prints in three albums, 1955–56.

In a number of innovative photo essays produced for *Life* magazine in the 1940s, such as "The Country Doctor," and "The Spanish Village," W. Eugene Smith helped establish the role of photographer as social commentator and author. His uncommissioned three-volume study of Pittsburgh, produced under a grant from the Guggenheim Foundation in the mid-1950s, presents a portrait of an American industrial city in a critical period in its history. The study includes about 750 proofs, many of which bear the editing marks of the photographer. *(Transfer, U.S. Copyright Office)*

Alfred Stieglitz. *Lower Manhattan.* Platinum print, 1910.

The work of American modernists like Stieglitz projected a heroic image of the American city, preaching the gospel of urban civilization. To a Europe straining under the torrent of displaced farmworkers pouring into Berlin, Paris, Vienna, and other cities from a depressed countryside, American metropolises like New York and Chicago looked like successful models for a new order. *(Gift of Georgia O'Keeffe)*

Edward Ruscha. *Standard [station].* Color silkscreen, 1966.

The pervasive impact of the automobile on the landscape has not escaped American artists of the twentieth century. The "disposable" artifacts of consumption and media, from soup cans to service stations, have inspired such major figures as Andy Warhol, Roy Lichtenstein, and Edward Ruscha. Previously considered crass, trivial, or worse, these phenomena are now read as clues to deeper truths about American culture and society. *(Pennell Fund purchase)*

Defining Moments: A Chronology

THE PICTORIAL COLLECTIONS of the Library of Congress are the product of almost two centuries of collaboration between the Congress, an international community of creators and benefactors, and the people of the United States. There have been a number of moments in the course of building this great national legacy when, aided by the initiative of individuals or organizations, the Library has set a bold new course in its mission of assembling and preserving a record of the past.

The origins of the Library's collections are traced to the acquisition by the Congress in 1815 of Thomas Jefferson's library, offered by the former president to replace the original congressional library burned by British troops during the War of 1812. Jefferson's library reflected his own legendary breadth of interests, including architecture and the fine arts, and thereby established a domain for the national library far broader than the primarily legislative and judicial interests of the original library.

The copyright act of 1870 centralized all U.S. copyright activity in the Library of Congress, and the Library became the sole repository of works copyrighted in America. Copyright law came about in the eighteenth century to afford statutory protection to creators against unauthorized copying and exploitation of their literary and artistic works. The books, prints, photographs, posters, architectural drawings, and other sorts of graphic works deposited for copyright registration came to form the foundation of the Library's American holdings.

In 1898 Gertrude M. Hubbard gave to the Library the distinguished collection of European and American prints formed by her late husband, American industrialist Gardiner Greene Hubbard. Hubbard's collection included old master prints from the sixteenth century onward, by such eminent figures as Dürer, Rembrandt, and Marcantonio Raimondi, as well as prints by more contemporary artists like Whistler, Meryon, and Seymour Haden. In its time the collection was one of the finest private holdings in the United States and Hubbard's gift established the Library of Congress as a national print cabinet.

In 1917 American printmaker, illustrator, and critic Joseph Pennell donated to the Library his extensive collection of the prints, drawings, and letters of the American artist James McNeill Whistler. Two years later Pennell made the Library the primary beneficiary of his estate, bequeathing to it the major portion of his own oeuvre, along with his assets and royalty income. In his desire to form a national collection of modern printmaking at the Library, Pennell specified that funds from his estate be used to purchase prints by Whistler, by living artists, or by artists who, in his words, "have produced art during the last 100 years." The impressive record of collecting compiled by the Pennell Committee for over sixty years has ensured that Pennell's legacy has continued to shape the Library's modern print holdings.

In 1926 the Library acquired its first master photographs: two important groups of works from the estate of influential pictorialist Clarence White and from fellow Photo-Secessionist Gertrude Käsebier. Although the Library had by this time amassed substantial holdings in documentary photographs, these acquisitions marked its recognition of the artistic value of the medium.

In the 1930s, the Carnegie Corporation provided funds to establish and support at the Library a national repository for photographic negatives of early American architecture, now called the Pictorial Archives of Early American Architecture. This development was encouraged by deposit at the Library in 1929 of several thousand photographic negatives of gardens and architectural subjects by one of the nation's finest architectural photographers, Frances Benjamin Johnston. This deposit was to be followed by many others in subsequent years. In turn, supported by a series of grants by the Carnegie Corporation, Johnston was commissioned by the Library to create an archive of her splendid photographs of the rapidly disappearing antebellum architecture of the American South. Johnston's donation of a body of her work set an important precedent for donations of architectural photographs by photographers, their families, and their sponsors, among them Gertrude Wittemann, Theodor Horydczak, Carol M. Highsmith, and Joseph E. Seagram and Sons.

In 1932 William Patten, art editor for *Harper's* Magazine during the 1880s and 1890s, initiated a multiyear campaign to assemble under the Library's roof the works of the golden age of American illustration. Patten's campaign of solicitations resulted in gifts to the Library by surviving artists or their descendants of the works of over two hundred American illustrators active in the period 1870 through World War I. Drawings were donated by such luminaries as Charles Dana Gibson, Howard Pyle, Alice Barber Stephens, and Elizabeth Shippen Green. In

1991 a bequest from Elizabeth Bendiner established the Alfred and Elizabeth Bendiner Memorial Fund to further augment the Library's collections in this area.

In 1933, largely through the efforts of Charles E. Peterson of the National Park Service, the Historic American Buildings Survey (HABS) was founded to aid unemployed architects and draftsmen. At the same time the survey was to produce through photographs, measured drawings, and written documentation a detailed record of early American architecture. The Library of Congress became the repository of the documentation and a partner in the administration of a program still very much active today. Joined in 1969 by the Historic American Engineering Record (HAER), HABS has recorded over 30,000 sites, structures, and artifacts.

In 1944 the combined archives of two landmark photographic documentation projects carried out successively within two federal agencies, the Farm Security Administration (FSA) and the Office of War Information (OWI), were placed by executive order under the administration of the Library of Congress. To the Library's already extensive pictorial coverage of American buildings, cities, and news events the FSA-OWI archive added an unparalleled record of the everyday experience of a broad spectrum of Americans in the period 1935–43.

In 1978 the Swann Collection of Caricature and Cartoons was donated to the Library by the Swann Foundation. During the 1950s and 1960s several dozen American editorial cartoonists, including Edwin Marcus of the *New York Times* and Clifford Berryman of the *Washington Star,* had donated their drawings to the Library. The Swann Collection, however, enlarged the scope of the Library's coverage of the history of caricature and political satire and provided a sound footing for the documentation of contemporary and historical uses of these genres. The Caroline and Erwin Swann Memorial Fund has continued to support the preservation and development of the collections of political cartoons and caricature as well as related publications and exhibits.

The 1989 bequest by Ray Eames of the Work of Charles and Ray Eames provided the Library with its first comprehensive archive of a design firm whose activity extended into almost every product of human creativity: films, architecture, industrial design, exhibitions, furniture, books, and graphic works. The influence of the Eameses on twentieth-century design has been profound, not only through their individual works but also through their working methods.